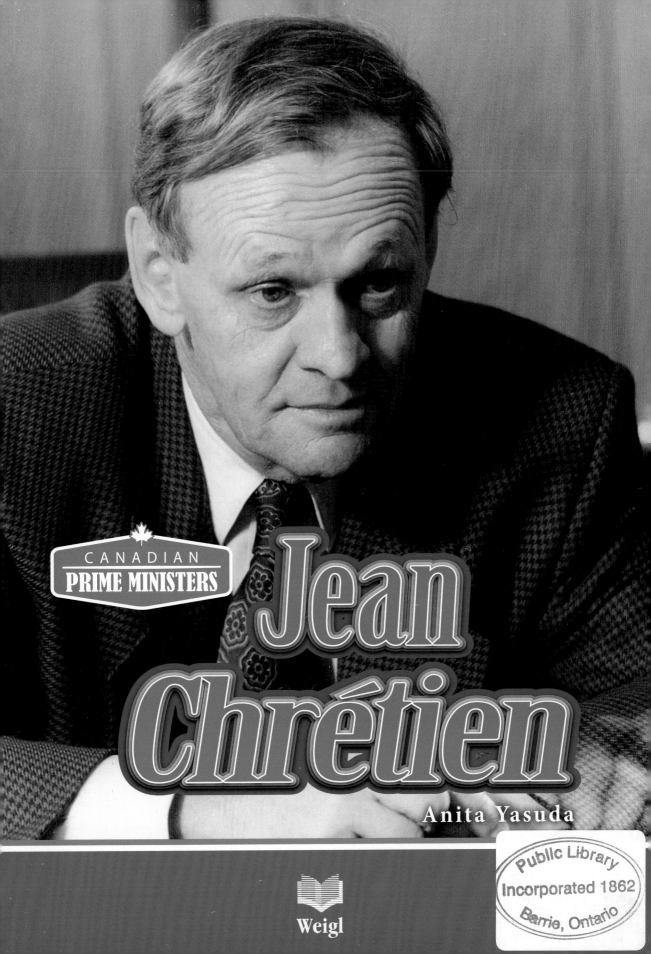

CANADIAN
PRIME MINISTERS

Jean Chrétien

Anita Yasuda

Weigl

Published by Weigl Educational Publishers Limited

6325 – 10th Street SE

Calgary, Alberta, Canada

T2H 2Z9

Website: www.weigl.ca

Library and Archives Canada Cataloguing in Publication

Yasuda, Anita, author

     Jean Chrétien / Anita Yasuda.

(Canadian prime ministers)

Issued in print and electronic formats.

ISBN 978-1-4872-0296-5 (bound).--ISBN 978-1-4872-0297-2 (pbk.).--

ISBN 978-1-4872-0298-9 (ebook)

     1. Chrétien, Jean, 1934- --Juvenile literature. 2. Canada--Politics

and government--1993-2006--Juvenile literature. 3. Prime ministers--

Canada--Biography--Juvenile literature. I. Title.

FC636.C47Y37 2015   j971.064'8092   C2015-901091-8

                                      C2015-901092-6

Printed in the United States of America in Brainerd, Minnesota

1 2 3 4 5 6 7 8 9 0 19 18 17 16 15

082015

100815

Editor: Heather Kissock

Design: Dean Pickup

We acknowledge the financial support of the Government of Canada through the Canada Book Fund for our publishing activities.

Photograph Credits

We acknowledge Getty Images, Corbis, CP Images, iStock, Alamy, Library and Archives Canada, Dreamstime, and Mario Groleau (p. 8) as our primary image suppliers for this title.

Contents

Who Is Jean Chrétien?

Jean Chrétien became Canada's 20th prime minister on November 4, 1993. His rise to this position was the culmination of a long career in politics. Chrétien was first elected to the House of Commons in 1963. He quickly gained a reputation for his informal manner and ability to connect with Canadians of all backgrounds.

From a young age, politics fascinated Chrétien. He studied law in order to pursue a political career. During his almost 40 years in the **federal** government, Chrétien was elected to Parliament 10 times. He held many **cabinet** positions, ranging from minister of Indian and Northern Affairs to minister of Justice. Chrétien served as leader of the Liberal Party of Canada from 1990 until 2003. He led the Liberals to three back-to-back victories, serving as prime minister for more than 10 years.

As prime minister of Canada, Chrétien worked to improve the country's **economy**. He did this by balancing the budget and eliminating the **deficit**. Chrétien also organized several international trade missions to expand Canada's economic reach. In 2003, Chrétien stepped down as prime minister and returned to practising law.

"A prime minister has a unique duty to preserve the integrity of the office. It is not about power. It is about responsibility."

Growing Up

Joseph Jacques Jean Chrétien was born on January 11, 1934. He was the 18th child born to Marie Boisvert and Wellie Chrétien. The family lived in Shawinigan, Quebec. Wellie was an outgoing man who worked in a paper mill. Marie, who was just as energetic as her husband, cared for their large family. Of the 19 children born to the couple, 10 died in infancy.

Jean's family was loving and supportive. His parents worked very hard to provide for their children. Marie grew food for the family in her vegetable garden. Wellie took on extra work installing generators for the local power company and selling insurance. Both Wellie and Marie had great ambitions for their children. What little money they were able to save was put aside for their children's education.

Shawinigan is nicknamed "The City of Energy" because of its location along the Saint-Maurice River. The river provides hydroelectric power for the province.

Get to Know Quebec

FLOWER

Blue Flag Iris

TREE

Yellow Birch

BIRD

Snowy Owl

QUEBEC

CAPITAL CITY
QUEBEC CITY

About 80 percent of all Quebecers speak French as their first language.

Quebec has more than 500,000 lakes, along with thousands of other waterways.

Approximately 80 percent of Quebecers live along the St. Lawrence River.

One of the world's largest hydroelectric power stations is located in Quebec's James Bay region.

Quebec City's Winter Carnival is held every year. Its mascot is a snowman called Bonhomme Carnaval.

Practice Makes Perfect

From an early age, Jean loved sports. He was small for his age and had a hearing impairment, but this did not stop him from taking charge. He loved to organize neighbourhood games. While Jean played hard, he struggled at school. One of the first schools he attended was Jardin de l'Enfance, a boarding school run by nuns. Jean hated the strict boarding school and begged his parents to take him home, but they said no. His father believed the structure the nuns provided would help Jean focus on his studies.

Jean later went on to attend the seminary college in Joliette and St. Joseph Seminary in Trois-Rivières. It was during this time that Jean began to dream of becoming a lawyer. He realized, however, that he would have to study harder if he wanted to be accepted into law school. He began applying himself to his studies more than ever before. In his final year at St. Joseph, he learned that he had been accepted into Laval University.

Trois-Rivières' St. Joseph Seminary was founded in 1860. Originally created to be a private school for boys, it opened to girls in 1998.

In the fall of 1955, Chrétien began studying law at Laval University. He had many friends and was president of the Liberal Club. Chrétien's peers recognized him as a natural-born politician. When he was not in class, Chrétien was busy engaging in political debates with fellow students.

Located in Quebec City, Laval was North America's first French language university.

Quick Facts

When Chrétien was 12 years old, he was stricken with a condition called Bell's palsy. The illness left part of his face paralyzed.

Chrétien shares a birthday with John A. Macdonald, Canada's first prime minister. Both men were born on January 11.

Chrétien was the first prime minister to win three consecutive majorities since 1945.

As minister of Justice, Chrétien appointed Bertha Wilson as Canada's first female Supreme Court justice.

Chrétien has been known to play the trombone on occasion. In fact, the Liberal **caucus** once gave him a trombone as a Christmas present.

After Chrétien graduated from Laval University, he returned to Shawinigan to practise law until he could enter politics. At the age of 29, Chrétien ran for the **riding** of Saint-Maurice-Laflèche. In April 1963, he was elected to the House of Commons. Chrétien quickly set out to learn about the workings of government and improve his English.

As minister of Indian Affairs and Northern Development, Chrétien visited Aboriginal communities across the country to meet the people and listen to their concerns.

Chrétien's drive got him noticed. In 1967, Prime Minister Lester Pearson made Chrétien a **minister without portfolio**. The following year, Chrétien became minister of National Revenue and then minister of Indian Affairs and Northern Development. Over the next two decades, Chrétien held several cabinet positions, allowing him to learn more about the issues facing the country. In 1990, Chrétien ran for the Liberal leadership and won on the first ballot. Three years later, he led the Liberals to a massive **majority government**, winning 177 seats of the available 295.

Chrétien played an integral role in creating the Canadian Charter of Rights and Freedoms. In 2012, he helped celebrate the charter's 30th anniversary at a rally in Toronto.

Thoughts from Jean Chrétien

During Jean Chrétien's 10 years as prime minister, he faced many challenges, within both Canada and the international community. Here are some of his comments on politics, his leadership style, and the issues facing governments around the world.

Chrétien comments on what it means to be in politics.

"To be frank, politics is about wanting power, getting it, exercising it, and keeping it. Helping people comes with it naturally, because you'll never be elected if you treat people badly."

Chrétien offers his thoughts on taking risks.

"To my mind, losing is always better than never trying, because you can never tell what may happen."

Chrétien discusses the challenges facing political leaders.

"The challenge we all face as leaders is how best to steer our governments' agenda back toward addressing the most critical problems facing our citizens. **Globalization** is certainly one factor affecting how democracies work."

Chrétien expresses his feelings toward his career.

"A man can't ask for much more than the chance to make a difference in his chosen field of work. Politics is my vocation. I'm forever grateful for the opportunity to contribute to this great country of ours. I know I am a better person for it."

What Is a Prime Minister?

A prime minister is the leader of a national government. This person represents the nation's citizens. The prime minister has many important responsibilities. One of these is choosing a cabinet. Members of the cabinet are each in charge of a particular government department, such as the Department of National Defence or the Department of Finance. They work closely with the prime minister to make decisions that are in the best interests of the country.

As prime minister, Chrétien attended the 2002 APEC Summit to discuss the economic issues facing Pacific Rim countries.

It takes hard work and dedication to become prime minister. This work continues once the position is attained. A prime minister must be willing to work long hours and keep up to date with the issues facing the country. He or she must also be able to communicate effectively with a variety of people.

A prime minister is responsible for maintaining relationships with key foreign partners. Chrétien often met with U.S. president George W. Bush to negotiate agreements between the two nations.

Prime Ministers 101

Louis Stephen St. Laurent
(1882–1973)

Louis St. Laurent was born in Compton, Quebec. He studied law at Laval University and graduated in 1905. St. Laurent had a long and successful law career before entering politics in 1941. He won the leadership of the Liberal Party in 1948 and became prime minister the same year. Under his leadership, Newfoundland became Canada's 10th province, and the St. Lawrence Seaway began construction.

Lester Bowles Pearson
(1939–1972)

Lester Pearson was born in Toronto, Ontario. After teaching history at the University of Toronto, he entered the field of **diplomacy**. He became minister of External Affairs in 1948. Pearson was Canada's leading diplomat in the 1950s and 1960s. He helped found the United Nations and, in 1957, won the Nobel Peace Prize. During his term as prime minister from 1963 to 1968, Pearson put in place a number of social programs that benefited Canadians.

Avril Kim Campbell
(1947–)

Kim Campbell was born in Port Alberni, British Columbia. She studied political science at the University of British Columbia. She then went on to the London School of Economics before returning to the University of British Columbia to study law. Campbell was elected to the federal government in 1988. She served as minister of Indian Affairs and Northern Development and minister of Justice. In 1993, Campbell became Canada's first female prime minister.

Stephen Harper
(1959–)

Stephen Harper was born in Toronto, Ontario. After graduating at the top of his high school class, he studied briefly at the University of Toronto before moving to Alberta. There, Harper worked for Imperial Oil and began attending the University of Calgary. In 1987, Harper became a founding member of the Reform Party. In 2004, he won the leadership of the Conservative Party of Canada. He became prime minister in 2006.

Influences

Chrétien's parents provided the foundation that led to his career in politics. When he was growing up, they encouraged him to think about others. They told him that he was not simply working to make life better for himself, but for the larger community. His parents raised him to believe that he had a responsibility to give back to society.

Wellie Chrétien dreamed that one of his sons would become a politician. A staunch Liberal supporter, Wellie had Jean help him hand out Liberal pamphlets during elections. He also took his teenage son to political rallies, where they listened to local politicians speak on the issues facing the community and the country.

Chrétien remembered the support Sharp had provided in his early years in politics. When Chrétien became prime minister, he invited Sharp to join his private staff and serve as an advisor.

Shortly after Chrétien arrived in Ottawa as a **member of Parliament (MP)**, he was assigned to be parliamentary secretary to Finance Minister Mitchell Sharp. Sharp took a particular interest in Chrétien. He spent many hours explaining to Chrétien how government worked. Sharp's advice was especially helpful to Chrétien when he later moved from **backbencher** to cabinet minister.

The Chrétien Family

Jean Chrétien met Aline Chaîné in Shawinigan while they were still teenagers. The couple dated for many years before marrying on September 10, 1957. The couple has three children. Their daughter France was born in 1958. Their son Hubert was born in 1965. The Chrétiens adopted their second son, Michel, in 1971.

Although a private person by nature, Aline Chrétien was by her husband's side through all of his election campaigns and victories.

Aline Chrétien has long been her husband's strongest supporter. Once the couple arrived in Ottawa, Aline worked on her English and taught herself how to speak Italian and Spanish. After her husband left public office, Aline continued to be involved in charity work. In 2010, she was made the first chancellor of Laurentian University in Ontario.

Overcoming Obstacles

When Chrétien became an MP in Ottawa, he spoke very little English. To become more comfortable with the language, he began reading English magazines and carried a dictionary with him. His facial paralysis sometimes interfered with his speech, but this did not stop him from expressing his opinions. Chrétien's determination to be a good politician caught the attention of then Prime Minister Lester Pearson. In 1967, he asked Chrétien to join his cabinet.

Chrétien faced more challenges as prime minister of Canada. In 2003, the governments of the United States and the United Kingdom launched military attacks on Iraq. These governments believed that Iraq had nuclear weapons that it was planning to use to help terrorists. They wanted to send military forces to destroy Iraq's nuclear weapons and depose Iraq's leader, Saddam Hussein.

Chrétien received a standing ovation in the House of Commons when he announced that Canada would not participate in the Iraq War.

Chrétien refused to send Canadian troops to Iraq. He wanted proof that Iraq had weapons of mass destruction before he would endorse a military mission. Some Canadians criticized Chrétien. Many Americans felt that Canada was not doing enough to help battle terrorism. Chrétien held firm. Instead, Canada sent troops to Afghanistan as part of a **NATO**-led mission. There, they worked with other countries to help free the Afghani people from the control of the Taliban government.

The Taliban was known to support the terrorist group al-Qaeda. Its former leader, Osama bin Laden, organized the 2001 attack on New York's World Trade Center.

Controversy followed Chrétien even after he left office. In 1996, Chrétien's government began a program to promote national unity in Quebec. The program ran until 2004. However, over time, it became clear that approximately $100 million of the program's funding had been misused. Some went to advertising agencies with ties to the Liberal Party. An inquiry was held. It found Chrétien partially responsible for the sponsorship scandal. However, this decision was overturned in 2008, and Chrétien was cleared of any wrongdoing.

The Gomery Commission was set up to investigate the sponsorship scandal. Chrétien testified before the commission on February 8, 2005.

Achievements and Successes

Canada had a multi-billion dollar deficit when Chrétien took office in 1993. He made it a priority to turn the country's economy around. By cutting government spending, he was able to eliminate Canada's deficit and create a surplus. Chrétien also promoted Canadian business through his "Team Canada" foreign trade missions. The goal of these missions was to develop markets for Canadian businesses.

On December 16, 2002, Chrétien signed the Kyoto Protocol. In doing so, he agreed that Canada would work toward reducing its greenhouse gas emissions.

Chrétien invited Canadian business leaders to accompany him on trips abroad. They would then meet with business leaders in other countries and work toward selling their goods and services.

In 1995, a nationwide **referendum** was held to decide whether Quebec would separate from the rest of Canada. When the results were counted, the 'No' forces won against Quebec separatists, but the vote was close. This concerned Chrétien's government. It wanted to ensure that a process was in place if a province decided it no longer wanted to be part of Canada. In 2000, Chrétien's government passed the Clarity Act. It outlined conditions that had to be met for a province to leave Canada.

Chrétien continues to be active, serving on committees, giving speeches, and writing articles and books. In 2007, he was given the Order of Canada, the country's highest civilian award. Two years later, Queen Elizabeth II honoured Chrétien's achievements in public service by presenting him with the Order of Merit. In 2012, Prime Minister Stephen Harper appointed Chrétien as the Canadian representative to the Diamond Jubilee Trust. The trust honours Queen Elizabeth II's 60 years on the throne. In this role, Chrétien helped to raise millions of dollars for charities across the **Commonwealth**.

Helping Others

When a prime minister retires from public service, **scholarships** are often created in his or her name. In 2003, the University of Ottawa established the Jean Chrétien Scholarship to honour Chrétien's long and distinguished career in politics. Each year, the university awards $5,000 to five of its students who are studying political science or public administration. To learn more about the Jean Chrétien scholarships, visit https://socialsciences.uottawa.ca/content/jean-Chrétien-scholarship

With a student population of more than 40,000, the University of Ottawa is the world's largest bilingual university.

Write a Biography

A person's life story can be the subject of a book. This kind of book is called a biography. Biographies describe the lives of remarkable people, such as those who have achieved great success or have done important things to help others. These people may be alive today, or they may have lived many years ago. Reading a biography can help you learn more about a remarkable person.

At school, you might be asked to write a biography. First, decide who you want to write about. You can choose a prime minister, such as Jean Chrétien, or any other person. Then, find out if your library has any books about this person. Learn as much as you can about him or her. Write down the key events in this person's life. What was this person's childhood like? What has he or she accomplished? What are his or her goals? What makes this person special or unusual?

A concept web is a useful research tool. Read the questions in the following concept web. Answer the questions in your notebook. Your answers will help you write a biography.

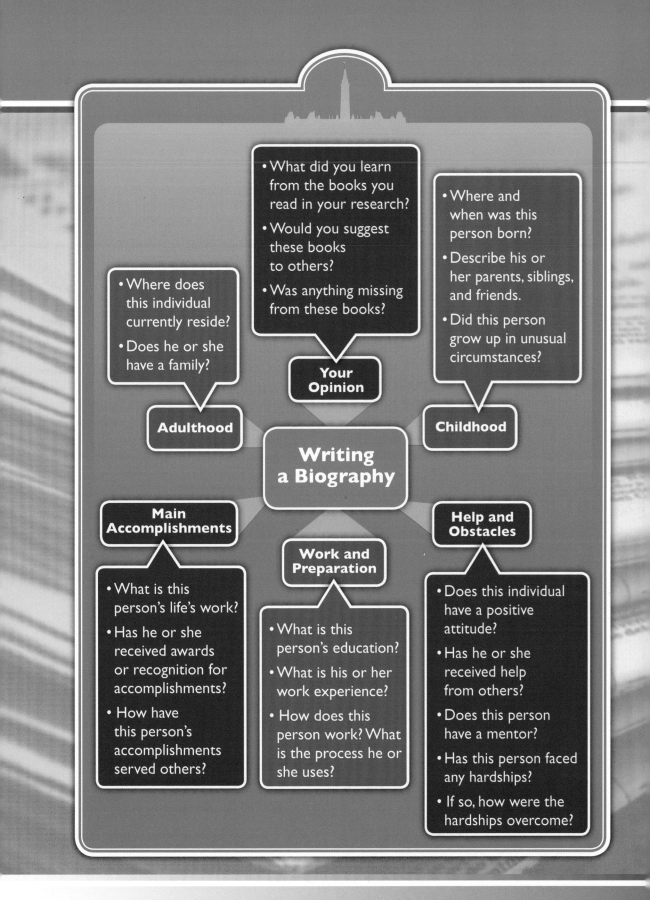

- What did you learn from the books you read in your research?
- Would you suggest these books to others?
- Was anything missing from these books?

Your Opinion

- Where and when was this person born?
- Describe his or her parents, siblings, and friends.
- Did this person grow up in unusual circumstances?

Childhood

- Where does this individual currently reside?
- Does he or she have a family?

Adulthood

Writing a Biography

Main Accomplishments

- What is this person's life's work?
- Has he or she received awards or recognition for accomplishments?
- How have this person's accomplishments served others?

Work and Preparation

- What is this person's education?
- What is his or her work experience?
- How does this person work? What is the process he or she uses?

Help and Obstacles

- Does this individual have a positive attitude?
- Has he or she received help from others?
- Does this person have a mentor?
- Has this person faced any hardships?
- If so, how were the hardships overcome?

Timeline

Year	Jean Chrétien	World Events
1934	Joseph Jacques Jean Chrétien is born on January 11 in Shawinigan, Quebec.	Adolf Hitler becomes the leader of Germany.
1958	Chrétien earns a law degree from Laval University.	Charles de Gaulle becomes the president of France.
1963	Chrétien wins the riding of Saint-Maurice-Laflèche, Quebec.	Martin Luther King, Jr. delivers his "I Have a Dream" speech at a civil rights rally in Washington, D.C.
1977	Chrétien becomes the first French-speaking minister of Finance.	Queen Elizabeth II celebrates her Silver Jubilee, signifying 25 years on the throne.
1980	Prime Minister Pierre Trudeau appoints Chrétien minister of Justice.	Ronald Reagan wins the U.S. presidential election.
1984	Chrétien becomes deputy prime minister and secretary of state for External Affairs.	Prime Minister Indira Gandhi of India is assassinated.
1990	Chrétien becomes leader of the Liberal Party and leader of the **Official Opposition**.	Iraqi troops invade Kuwait.
1993	After winning the federal election, Chrétien is sworn in as prime minister on November 4.	A treaty between 12 states creates the European Union.
2003	Chrétien steps down as prime minister.	The United States and the United Kingdom launch a war against Iraq.

Further Resources

To find out more about Jean Chrétien, visit the following websites. Other reputable websites usually include government sites, educational sites, and online encyclopedias.

Listen to an analysis of Chrétien's political career at www.prime-ministers.ca/chretien/bio_1.php

Read more about Jean Chrétien's life at www.thecanadianencyclopedia.ca/en/article/joseph-jacques-jean-chretien

Watch Jean Chrétien discuss Canada–United States relations at www.c-span.org/video/?301110-1/uscanada-relations

Key Words

backbencher: a member of Parliament who does not hold government office

cabinet: a select group of people who advise the prime minister

caucus: all members of a political party in Parliament

Commonwealth: a voluntary association of 53 countries, most of which were once ruled by Great Britain

deficit: when a government spends more than it brings in

diplomacy: the skill of dealing with people sensitively and effectively

economy: the management of a country's wealth and resources

federal: government at the national level

globalization: a situation in which available goods and services gradually become similar in all parts of the world

majority government: a governing party that has more than half the total number of seats in the House of Commons

member of Parliament (MP): someone who has been elected to the House of Commons

minister without portfolio: a member of the cabinet who does not head a department

NATO: the North Atlantic Treaty Organization, a military alliance between the United States, Canada, and numerous European countries

Official Opposition: the party with the second-highest number of votes

referendum: a vote on a political question

riding: a geographical area represented by a member of Parliament

scholarships: payments given to support a student's education

Index

Emma saw that Mama had hung quilts separating the sleeping places from the cooking and eating place. She put Hannah down near a sleeping place.

"You can unpack that box over there." Mama pointed to the cooking and eating place. "Everything needs to be put away. Tomorrow is a workday. Tomorrow is apple picking."

Emma emptied one box and started the next. Mama's hard-times jar lay tucked between blankets. It was just about half full of loose change. Solid nickels. Rusty red pennies. Thin dimes. And every now and then a fat quarter.

"What are we going to do with all this money?" Emma knew before she asked. She just wanted to make double sure.

"That money being saved in case we run out of something important before payday," Mama informed her.

"That's why she call it the hard-times jar. 'Cause it's for hard times," Robert Earl said. He was silent for a quick minute, then added, "Bet I know what Emma would do with all that money. She'd buy her a real book. Wouldn't you, Emma?"

"No extras," Mama said as she went about her busyness.

"No extras," Robert Earl repeated.

"No extras," Emma whispered to the hard-times jar.

The next morning, while darkness still filled the windows, Daddy nudged Emma.

"Time to roll out with your working clothes on," he whispered.

When Emma pushed through the quilt curtain, Mama pointed to the corner. "The wash pan over yonder. And your plate waiting."

Emma dabbed the washcloth over her face and passed it on. "Here, Robert E., wash."

"Roll out with your working clothes on," Robert said, waving the cloth at Hannah.

"Robert Earl, don't bother with Hannah. Wash." Mama's head was already wrapped for work. "Emma, eat. And we'll leave for the orchard."

"We taking red beans and rice for lunch?" Emma asked, her words full of cornbread.

"Red beans and rice," said Mama.

"Everybody ready? Apple-picking time," said Daddy, grabbing the box of food.

Before sunshine spread through the trees, Daddy laid his extra-long ladder in their branches. All the way to the top he climbed, picking high above Emma's head. Mama seated Hannah in an empty crate. She pulled apples that hung down low.

"Apple-picking time," she said, turning to Emma.

Emma had already picked herself one. It tasted of morning, cool and crisp. Emma licked the sweetness dripping down her chin.

Robert Earl gathered red fruit off the ground. "Some of these all gushy," he said with a mouthful of apple.

"Pick only the good drops from under the tree," Daddy told him.

Daddy's large sack quickly bulged running-over full. He released the strap, and round redness rushed into crates with loud thuds.

The sound of spilling apples gave Emma another idea. She needed one minute. *Lizzy tumbled over and over, stomach hard as bricks . . .* Emma pulled out a piece of brown paper and scribbled.

"Emma. Emma Jean!" Mama called from between the branches. "Do you want me to hide that pencil?"

That was the last thing Emma wanted. She slid the pencil and paper back in her pocket. She piled apples high in the crate. She'd work plenty to add money to the hard-times jar. That way there'd be some left over for extras. That way she'd get a store-bought book.

Sometime after the sun climbed over the tip of Daddy's ladder, Mama passed red beans and rice. Emma set her tin plate down and scribbled, . . . *all the other lizards around Lizzy—they got pukey-green sick, too.* She wrote in between mouthfuls. *And that's why lizards are green instead of brown.* Emma dabbed the pencil on her tongue. *The End,* she finished. Emma turned the paper over. She'd planned on making up another story right then. But Daddy called that it was time for work again.

One evening, when the trees in the orchard grew thin shadows, Mama sat Emma down.

"Emma Jean," she began, "tomorrow you won't be picking apples."

"I won't?" Emma's eyes filled with tears. How could she add money to the hard-times jar? How could she ever earn enough for extras if she didn't go to the orchard? "I have to," Emma cried.

"I'm sorry," Mama told her. "But you'll be going to school."

"School?" Emma frowned. "I never went to school before when we came up on the season." That's what some folks called coming up north to work the crops. "Why can't I just wait until we get back to Florida? Please," Emma begged.

"I know how you feel. But you're eight now. You shouldn't be missing any school," Mama said, hugging Emma's shoulders.

The very next morning Emma stood at the end of the dirt road. Her stomach felt all squiggly.

"You'll be fine," Mama told her as the bus drove up.

But she didn't feel fine. She wished she was back at the orchard as the bus stopped in front of the red-brick school.

"You must be Emma," a lady said, meeting her at the door.

"Yes, ma'am," Emma nodded.

"I'm Miss Miller, the third-grade teacher," she said, her lips curving into a smile.

Emma looked down and watched her foot move back and forth. She didn't like being eight anymore. And she didn't like Pennsylvania either.

"You'll like my classroom," Miss Miller assured her. "We have lots of girls and boys your age."

Miss Miller's face reminded Emma of buttermilk, all creamy and white. "Come along." She took Emma's hand. "Let's go in."

Emma walked into the third-grade room. There were lots of boys and girls just like Miss Miller had said. But none were chocolate-brown like her. They all looked like Miss Miller. Emma's stomach felt squiggly. She had never gone to school with people Miss Miller's color. Down south it was not allowed. Down south it was against the law.

"Emma," Miss Miller said, "let me show you around." Miss Miller led the way. Her hair was rolled at the back like a thick doughnut.

"This is our coatroom," she told Emma. "And this"—she pulled back a curtain to another room—"is our library."

Emma's eyes grew larger than quarters. Books. Walls and walls of books. From the floor halfway to the ceiling—books. The store-bought kind.

"You may read any of these books," Miss Miller told her. "None can be taken home," she cautioned, "but you are free to read as much as you want during activity period."

"Honest?" Emma asked.

"Honest," Miss Miller promised.

And that afternoon, when Miss Miller announced activity period, she told the class they could work on arts and crafts or choose books from the library.